THE AMAZING BOOK OF

LEGO® STAR WARS™

Written by David Fentiman

Introduction

Have you ever met an Ewok, or seen the Empire's mighty Death Star? Have you faced the scary rancor, or joined the brave Jedi Knights? All of this and much, much more awaits you. Welcome to the amazing LEGO® *Star Wars*™ galaxy.

Look out for **fun questions** throughout the book.

CONTENTS

JEDI MASTERS

Yoda

Master Yoda is the wise and powerful leader of the Jedi. He is hundreds of years old. Like all Jedi, he can use a mysterious power called the Force.

Jedi robes

Green skin

Pointy ears

Purple lightsaber

Mace Windu

Mace Windu is one of the bravest Jedi Masters. He leads the Jedi alongside Yoda. The Force makes him strong and fast.

Obi-Wan Kenobi

Obi-Wan used to be Qui-Gon's apprentice. Now, this wise and caring Jedi Master trains his own apprentice, named Anakin.

Lift the flap to see him!

Have you met my apprentice?

Pilot headset

Qui-Gon Jinn

Qui-Gon Jinn is a skilled Jedi and fearless fighter, but Yoda worries that he doesn't always think before he acts.

If you were a Jedi, what color would your lightsaber be?

Blue lightsaber

Darth Sidious

The leader of the Sith is named Darth Sidious. This sneaky villain wants to defeat the Jedi and rule the galaxy.

Force lightning shoots from fingertips

Scarred face

Head horns

Double-bladed lightsaber

Darth Maul

Darth Maul is Sidious's first apprentice. He is fearsome, with sharp horns on his head and fangs instead of teeth.

6

SINISTER SITH

Sith cloak

Darth Vader
Powerful Darth Vader has robot arms and legs, and wears a mask that hides his face. He is Darth Sidious's final apprentice.

Face mask

Robotic arm

Which Sith do you think is the scariest?

Mon Calamari

Mon Calamari can live both on land and under the sea! They have thick, rubbery skin to keep the water out.

Rebel uniform

Eyes can see underwater

Glowing plasma spear

Energy shield

Utility belt

Gungans

The honorable Gungans come from a green planet called Naboo. They are great warriors, and live in cities at the bottom of a lake.

AMAZING ALIENS

Wings flap very fast

Lift the flap to see them!

Would you like to meet the Ewoks?

Eyes are on stalks

Sonic blaster

Geonosians

Geonosians look like giant insects. They live in big hives, and are very good at building droids.

Armored skin

Ewoks

These cute-looking creatures are actually brave hunters. They live in tribes on the Forest Moon of Endor.

Leather clothing

Headdress made from a bird skull

Fur has turned gray with age

Chief's staff

Spear used
for hunting

Ewok fur
comes in
lots of colors

Ears can
hear long
distances

Bow made
from strong
wood

Medicine
bag

Blaster

Battle droid

Basic battle droids are not very smart, but they are cheap and easy to build.

Robot legs

Photoreceptor eye

Droideka

Deadly droidekas have perfect aim with their powerful blasters. They can transform into a ball shape and roll toward their targets.

Spiky legs fold up

Disk-shaped body

Droid gunship

Speedy droid gunships zoom over the battlefield, firing their missiles at the Jedi.

Missile launcher

Antenna

Tank droid

Tank droids are big, heavy fighting machines. Their thick armor protects them from blasters and missiles.

Tank track

Heavy blaster

Jawa

Jawas are small creatures that live on the desert planet, Tatooine. They search the sand dunes for junk to sell, and steal anything they can find!

Glowing orange eyes

Ion blaster for disabling droids

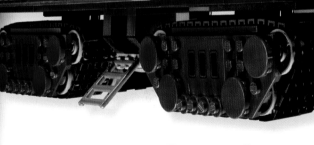

Jawa sandcrawler

Jawas travel across the desert in this huge vehicle. It has wide tracks so that it doesn't get stuck in the sand.

Staff is called a gaffi stick

Claw for grabbing junk

Front opens to make a ramp

Tusken Raider

Tusken Raiders are very fierce. They wear scary masks, and attack anyone they come across.

What would you like to **build** out of recycled **junk?**

13

ANAKIN SKYWALKER

When I grow up, I want to be a Jedi!

Lift the flap to see what happens!

Young Anakin

Anakin grows up on the planet Tatooine. He works for a mean junk trader named Watto. At first, Anakin doesn't realize he has Force powers.

Pilot controls

Anakin's podracer

Using spare parts, Anakin builds a podracer so he can enter a famous podracing contest. He beats the other pilots and wins the race!

Twin engines

C-3PO

Anakin is really good at building machines. He builds a smart droid, named C-3PO, to help his mother.

What kind of droid would you build?

Photoreceptor eye

Power recharging port

Gold plating

Air scoops

15

Cockpit

Astromech copilot droid

Colored yellow to match his childhood podracer

Anakin's starfighter

As a Jedi, Anakin has his own personal ship. It is a small and speedy starfighter, called a Jedi Interceptor.

Padawan Anakin

Anakin leaves Tatooine and becomes a Padawan, a Jedi apprentice. He trains for many years with Master Obi-Wan Kenobi.

Pilot headset

Jedi tunic

Jedi Anakin

Finally, Anakin passes the tests to become a Jedi Knight. He takes part in many daring missions to protect the Galactic Republic.

WEIRD CREATURES

Tentacles for grabbing prey

Sarlacc

This giant creature hides most of its body under Tatooine's desert sand. Its gaping mouth gobbles up anything that gets too close.

Fangs stop prey escaping

Eye on a stalk

Dianoga

The dianoga looks like a huge squid. It lives in junk piles, and grabs its food with its long, sticky tentacles.

Razor-sharp fangs

Rancor

The terrible rancor is a pet of the gangster Jabba the Hutt. It lives in the basement of Jabba's palace, and it is always hungry!

Huge claws

Key for rancor cage

Prod for controlling the rancor

Malakili

Malakili is the rancor's keeper. Everyone else thinks the rancor is a monster, but Malakili loves it anyway.

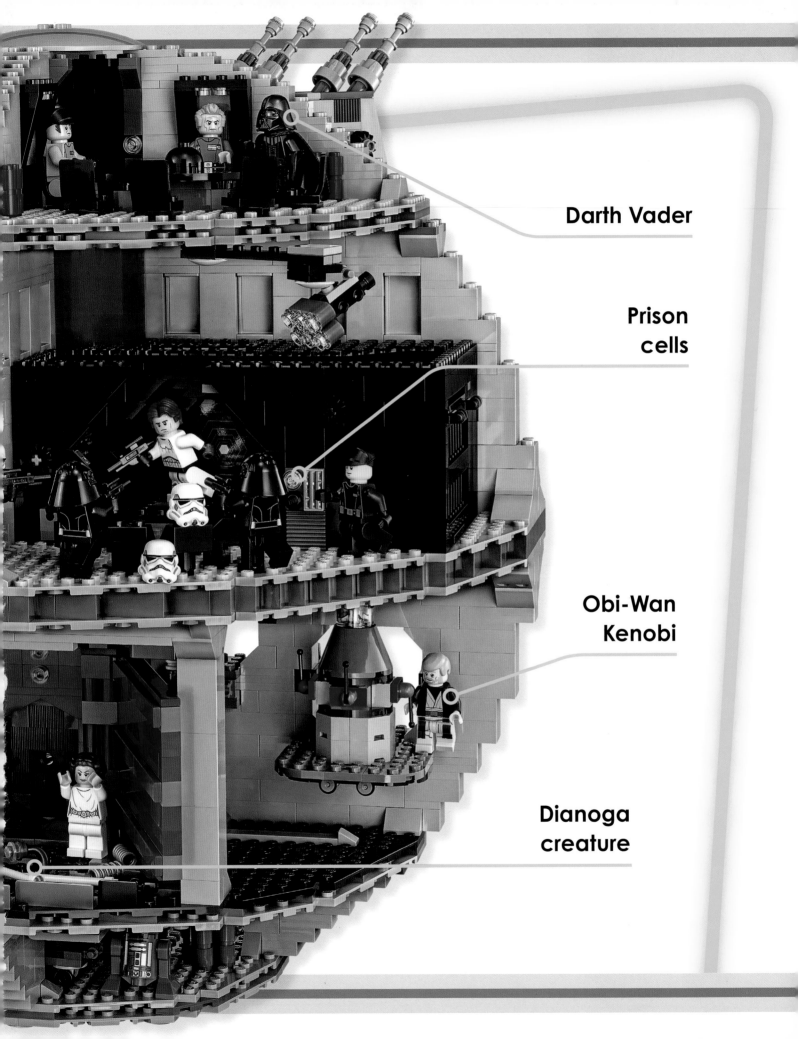

Darth Vader

Prison cells

Obi-Wan Kenobi

Dianoga creature

C-3PO

Superlaser

What would your **job** be on board the **Death Star?**

Death Star

The Death Star is the Empire's secret weapon. It looks like a giant ball, and it has a huge laser that it uses to blast planets!

The Emperor

The sneaky Emperor has taken over the galaxy, and turned it into the Empire. No one knows that he is really the evil Sith Lord, Darth Sidious!

Long, dark robes

Force pike

Face mask

Royal Guard

The Emperor has his own special bodyguards. They wear red cloaks and protect the Emperor from harm.

Imperial navy trooper

The Empire has a huge fleet of starships. Navy troopers work on board these massive ships, and on the Empire's Death Star.

Just wait until you see the Death Star!

Lift the flap to see it!

Trooper helmet

Rank badge

Imperial officer

Imperial officers are in charge of the Empire's powerful army. They always follow the Emperor's orders.

19

Stormtrooper

The Empire's scary soldiers are called stormtroopers. There are millions of them, all ready to fight the Empire's enemies.

Blaster pistol

Armor protects legs

Scout trooper

Scout troopers ride super-fast vehicles called speeder bikes. They are used to spy behind enemy lines.

Steering vanes

How would you escape from a scout trooper?

Speeder bike

Snowtrooper

Some stormtroopers are trained to fight on cold planets. They wear special armor to keep themselves warm.

Armor heating controls

Chain comes from Mon's home planet, Chandrilla

Mon Mothma

Mon Mothma is the wise leader of the Rebel Alliance. She created the Alliance to fight back against the evil Empire.

General Rieekan

General Rieekan is an experienced rebel soldier. He is in charge of the Alliance base on the icy planet Hoth.

Rebel uniform

Blaster pistol

Do you think Anakin can become good again?

Evil Anakin

Darth Vader is really Anakin Skywalker! The brave Jedi was tricked by Darth Sidious, and turned to the dark side of the Force.

Eyes turned yellow by the dark side

Cockpit hatch

TIE Advanced

Vader flies a special ship. It is a TIE fighter, but it is faster, tougher, and more powerful than all other TIE fighters.

Rubbery skin

Admiral Ackbar

Admiral Ackbar commands the rebel fleet. He is a Mon Calamari from the planet Mon Cala.

Princess Leia

Brave Princess Leia comes from the planet Alderaan. At first, she secretly spies for the Alliance. Later, she leads its soldiers in battle.

Lift the flap to see!

Years ago, I looked very different.

Dark armor

Darth Vader is kept alive by his armor. His arms and legs are now made of metal, and he wears a mask over his face.

DARTH VADER

Solar panels in wings

Vader duels Obi-Wan

When Darth Vader first turned bad, Obi-Wan Kenobi fought Vader and defeated him. Many years later, they battle again.

Old Jedi robes

Mask hides Vader's face

GREEDY GANGSTERS

Huge
mouth

Jabba the Hutt
Jabba the Hutt is a disgusting giant slug. This vile gang boss rules over the worst criminals in the galaxy.

Long,
slimy tail

Snout

Utility vest

Greedo
Nasty Greedo works for Jabba the Hutt. He hunts down people who have made Jabba angry.

Sharp teeth

Bib Fortuna

Beastly Bib Fortuna looks after Jabba's palace. He is also in charge of Jabba's gang of henchmen.

Head-tail, known as a lekku

Combat armor

Tasu Leech

The Kanjiklub is a scruffy gang of bandits. Its leader is a fearsome warrior named Tasu Leech.

27

Astromech copilot droid

X-wing

X-wings are the rebels' best starfighters. They are fast and have four powerful laser cannons.

Laser cannons on wingtips

Cockpit

Sensor dome

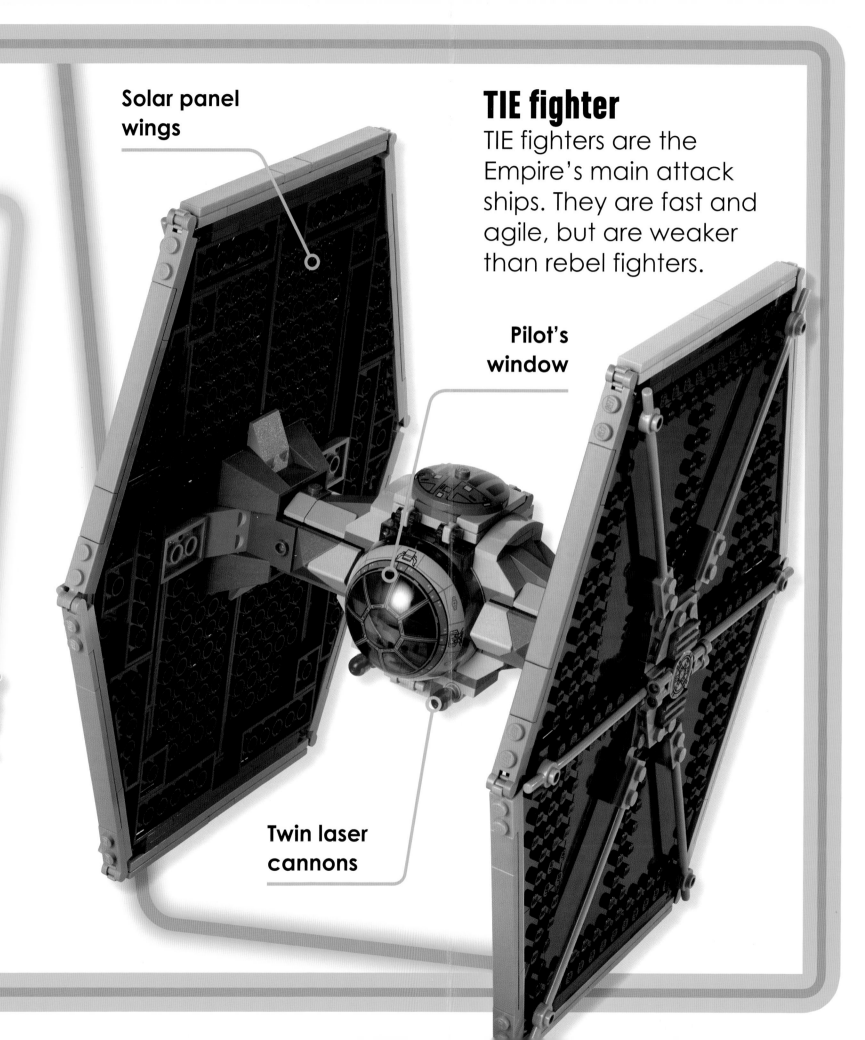

Which starfighter would you choose to fly?

Solar panel wings

TIE fighter

TIE fighters are the Empire's main attack ships. They are fast and agile, but are weaker than rebel fighters.

Pilot's window

Y-wing

Y-wings are slow, but they are very tough. They carry torpedoes to attack bigger ships.

Twin laser cannons

Ion jet engine

TIE pilot

Imperial pilots are well-trained and determined. They have the rebels outnumbered!

Lift the flap to see it!

My ship is faster than these!

BOUNTY HUNTERS

Helmet comes from the planet Mandalore

Targeting rangefinder

Boba Fett

Boba Fett was trained by his father, Jango. This ruthless warrior becomes the most feared bounty hunter of them all.

Blaster pistol

Jango Fett

Jango Fett is the best bounty hunter in the galaxy. He carries lots of tools and gadgets to help him with his job.

Combat armor

Scanners

Photoreceptor eye

Tall droid head

IG-88

Unlike other bounty hunters, this droid doesn't need to sleep or eat. This makes it extra-dangerous.

Scaly skin

Bossk

Bossk is a Trandoshan, a type of giant lizard. He is a fierce fighter, but he is also very honest. Bossk always keeps his promises.

Blaster rifle

MILLENNIUM FALCON

Cockpit on side of ship

Missile launchers

Legendary ship

The *Millennium Falcon* is very famous. It looks old and worn out, but it is the fastest ship in the galaxy!

Where would *you fly to in* the *Falcon*?

Laser turret

Han Solo

Han Solo is the owner of the *Millennium Falcon*. He often gets himself into tricky situations, but he is good at heart and always helps his rebel friends.

Leather jacket

Body is covered in fur

Wookiee bowcaster

Chewbacca

Chewbacca is Han Solo's loyal copilot. He is a Wookiee from the planet Kashyyyk.

WALKERS

AT-TE
Each AT-TE has six legs, and carries a large cannon on its back. These sturdy machines can even climb up vertical cliffs!

Heavy cannon

Cockpit

Insect-like legs

AT-TE driver
The Republic uses clone troopers to drive its walkers. These soldiers are all completely identical.

Lift the flap to see one!

Have you ever seen an AT-AT? They're huge!

Communications antenna

Shield protects driver

AT-RT

AT-RTs are small, agile walkers with only two legs. They can run very fast and jump over obstacles.

Ankle joint

Single laser cannon

Which walker would you like to drive?

Top hatch

Strong legs

Twin blaster cannons on walker's chin

AT-ST

AT-STs are smaller and faster than AT-ATs. The Empire uses them to catch rebels who try to escape.

Big feet keep walker steady

AT-AT

AT-ATs are the Empire's biggest walkers. Their heads hold powerful laser cannons and their bodies contain squads of stormtroopers.

Troop compartment

Neck can bend

Driver in cockpit

Knee joint

Horns

Wampa

Wampas are huge, fearsome hunters. They roam Hoth's snowdrifts, looking for things to eat.

Thick,
white fur

Goggles
protect eyes

Claws

Rebel Hoth trooper

Rebel soldiers on Hoth have to wear thick padded uniforms to keep themselves warm.

PLANET HOTH

Snowspeeder pilot

Blaster cannon

Snowspeeder
The swift rebel snowspeeder is designed to fly through Hoth's thin, icy air.

Saddle for rebel trooper

Tauntaun
On Hoth, some of the rebels' vehicles won't work in the snow. Instead, the rebels ride big, furry creatures called Tauntauns.

Reins

LUKE SKYWALKER

Luke's electrobinoculars

Tatooine Luke

Luke grows up on the planet Tatooine. He gets caught up in the battle against the Empire, and decides to join the rebels.

Rebel pilot helmet

Life-support system

Pilot Luke

Fearless Luke flies an X-wing into battle against the Empire. He uses it to defeat the Empire's secret weapon, the Death Star.

Green lightsaber replaces Luke's lost blue one

Jedi Luke

After escaping from the Empire on planet Hoth, Luke finds the Jedi Master, Yoda. Wise Yoda trains Luke to be a great Jedi.

Arms fold out of body

R2-D2

This friendly droid once belonged to Luke's father, Anakin. R2-D2 joins Luke on his adventures, and helps him fight the Empire.

REBELLIOUS REY

Quarterstaff

Scavenger Rey
Rey lives on the planet Jakku. She explores the desert looking for things to scavenge, and trades the things that she finds for food.

BB-8
On Jakku, Rey finds the droid BB-8 lost and alone, and they agree to team up. It turns out BB-8 is carrying top-secret information.

Saddle

Tools

Rey's speeder

Talented Rey has built her own speeder out of spare parts. It is fun to ride and very fast.

Luke Skywalker's old lightsaber

Powerful Rey

Rey realizes that she has amazing abilities, and decides to find Luke Skywalker. She hopes that he can train her to become a Jedi.

General Hux

The rebels beat the Empire, but it has returned as the First Order! General Hux leads the First Order's army. He has also built a new secret weapon, called the Starkiller.

First Order uniform

Captain Phasma

Fierce Captain Phasma commands the First Order's stormtroopers. She stands out on the battlefield in her suit of silver armor.

Kylo Ren

Kylo Ren is the First Order's greatest warrior. This fearsome fighter wants to battle Luke Skywalker and defeat him.

Lift the flap to see!

Shall I take off my mask?

Mask

Kylo's lightsaber

Rey versus Kylo

Rey uses Luke Skywalker's old lightsaber to duel with Kylo. Kylo is stronger, and his anger makes him powerful. It is a tough battle!

Kylo's special
lightsaber has
three blades

Who do
you think
will win?

Jakku
desert outfit

Luke
Skywalker's
lightsaber

Resistance symbol on Poe's helmet

Poe Dameron

Poe is the bravest and best pilot in the Resistance. No mission is too difficult or dangerous for Poe.

Cockpit

Laser cannon

Poe's X-wing

Poe flies a special black-and-orange X-wing. It is a modern version of the Rebel Alliance's X-wings.

Colors are unique to Poe's ship

BRAVE RESISTANCE

General Leia Organa

General Organa leads the Resistance against the First Order. She was one of the rebels who defeated the Empire.

Finn

Finn used to be a First Order stormtrooper. He decided to run away and join the Resistance instead. Now he fights for the good side!

Finn has borrowed Poe's jacket

1 What color is Mace Windu's lightsaber?

2 Who was Darth Sidious's first apprentice?

3 Which planet do Gungans come from?

4 What shape can droidekas transform into?

5 What kind of creature is this?

6 What is the name of the droid built by Anakin Skywalker?

7 Which creature hides beneath Tatooine's desert sand?

8 What color are the Emperor's Royal Guards?

9 What are the stormtroopers who fight on cold planets known as?

10 Who is this?

11 What kind of ship does Darth Vader fly?

QUIZ

12 What is the name of the leader of the Kanjiklub?

13 Which rebel starfighter has four powerful laser cannons?

14 Who is this?

15 Who owns the *Millennium Falcon*?

16 Which type of walker has six legs?

17 What are the furry creatures that the rebels ride on Hoth?

18 Where did Luke Skywalker grow up?

19 What is the name of the scavenger from Jakku?

20 Who is the First Order's greatest warrior?

You can find the answers on page 48.

Penguin Random House

Senior Editor David Fentiman
Senior Art Editor Jo Connor
Pre-production Producer Siu Chan
Senior Producer Lloyd Robertson
Managing Editor Paula Regan
Design Manager Jo Connor
Publisher Julie Ferris
Art Director Lisa Lanzarini
Publishing Director Simon Beecroft

Written by David Fentiman

First American Edition, 2017
Published in the United States by DK Publishing
345 Hudson Street, New York, New York 10014

Page design copyright © 2017 Dorling Kindersley Limited.
DK, a Division of Penguin Random House LLC
17 18 19 10 9 8 7 6 5 4 3 2 1
001–298131–Mar/17

A catalog record for this book is available from the Library of Congress.

ISBN 978-1-4654-5541-3

DK books are available at special discounts when purchased in bulk for
sales promotions, premiums, fund-raising, or educational use. For details,
contact: DK Publishing Special Markets, 345 Hudson Street, New York,
New York 10014
SpecialSales@dk.com

DK would like to thank Sam Bartlett for design assistance,
Randi Kirsten Sørensen, Paul Hansford, Martin Leighton Lindhardt, and
Heidi K. Jensen at the LEGO Group, and Jennifer Heddle at Lucasfilm.

Printed and bound in China

A WORLD OF IDEAS:
SEE ALL THERE IS TO KNOW

www.dk.com
www.LEGO.com/starwars
www.starwars.com

Answers to the quiz on pages 46 and 47:

1 Purple
2 Darth Maul
3 Naboo
4 A ball
5 Jawa
6 C-3PO
7 Sarlacc
8 Red
9 Snowtroopers
10 Princess Leia
11 TIE Advanced
12 Tasu Leech
13 X-wing
14 IG-88
15 Han Solo
16 AT-TE
17 Tauntauns
18 Tatooine
19 Rey
20 Kylo Ren